Roberto Clemente

Roberto Clemente

BASEBALL'S HUMANITARIAN HERO

Herón Márquez

 Carolrhoda Books, Inc./Minneapolis

Carolrhoda Books, Inc.
A division of Lerner Publishing Group
241 First Avenue North
Minneapolis, MN 55401 U.S.A.

Website address: www.carolrhodabooks.com

Library of Congress Cataloging-in-Publication Data

Márquez, Herón.
    Roberto Clemente : baseball's humanitarian hero / by Herón Márquez.
    p.   cm. — (Trailblazer biography)
    Includes bibliographical references and index.
    ISBN: 1–57505–767–0 (lib. bdg. : alk. paper)
    1. Clemente, Roberto, 1934–1972—Juvenile literature. 2. Baseball
players—Puerto Rico—Biography—Juvenile literature. I. Title. II. Series.
GV865.C45M37 2005
796.357'092—dc22   2004002319

Manufactured in the United States of America
1 2 3 4 5 6 – JR – 10 09 08 07 06 05

Contents

Roberto Clemente's sharp hitting and fast feet made him an excellent baseball player and a fan favorite.

Introduction

By the 1972 baseball season, Roberto Clemente had long been considered the greatest baseball player ever to come out of Puerto Rico. He had won many awards and was adored by the fans in Pittsburgh, Pennsylvania, where his team, the Pirates, played. With the Pirates, he had won two World Series championships, most recently the previous fall, in 1971. His performance in that World Series was one of the greatest displays of all-around playing ever seen in championship play. More important than his playing accomplishments was that he was a renowned humanitarian, dedicated to helping others. Already he was probably a shoe-in to be inducted into the National Baseball Hall of Fame.

But the 1972 season had carved a place for him among the immortals of the game. In 1972 Clemente had marched, one hit at a time, toward his 3,000th career hit—an important benchmark for a star major-league hitter.

By Saturday, September 30, 1972, Clemente had 2,999 hits, but only two games were left in the season. Even an

Clemente gets a hit at a game on September 26, 1972. The hit left Clemente just four short of his 3,000-hit goal.

outstanding batter can go hitless in two games. And the Pirates were playing the New York Mets, who had a strong pitching staff. Getting a hit against the Mets pitchers would not be easy.

The starting pitcher for New York that Saturday was an impressive young left-hander named Jon Matlack. Matlack struck out Clemente in the first inning. Then Clemente came up to bat again in the fourth inning. Matlack got ahead of Clemente with a first-pitch strike. The count was 0–1. His second pitch was a curveball, and Clemente cracked it into the outfield. The ball hit the grass and reached the fence in left-center field. The Mets center fielder threw it back to the infield, but Clemente was already standing on second base with a double. It was his 3,000th hit.

The crowd cheered long and hard, showing their appreciation and love for the ballplayer they knew as the Great One. Though he was shy in receiving such praise, Clemente stood on second base and soaked up the cheers. He was only the eleventh player in history to reach 3,000 hits. He was also the first Latino player to do it, which made the achievement all the more important. He had become an important symbol of everything that was good in Puerto Rico and in baseball. He had gone from being a dirt-poor boy who played baseball with sticks and balls made of rags to being one of the most popular athletes in the world. In his life and his career, he had carried himself with dignity. He had made his family, his fellow Puerto Ricans, and the game of baseball proud.

Baseball is very popular throughout the Caribbean region. Children use whatever they can find, such as sticks for bats and chalk-outlined bases, to play the sport.

chapter 1

FIELD OF DREAMS

Roberto Clemente's parents never had to worry where their son was when he wasn't home. They knew that if school was in session, he was busy learning. If school was not in session, he could be in only one place: playing baseball with his friends in a dirt field near their home in Carolina, Puerto Rico, an island in the Caribbean Sea. In fact, by the age of five, Roberto was already in love with baseball.

Roberto and his friends, who all grew up poor, used whatever they could find to make baseball equipment. Balls were made from cans, milk cartons, balled up rags, socks wrapped around golf balls, and old tennis balls. Brooms or tree branches became bats, and old coffee bags were bases.

The boys would take turns hitting, pitching, and fielding. The rules were simple: A player was allowed to stay up at bat until he struck out. After the strikeout, the pitcher would step up to bat. One of the fielders would take the pitcher's place while waiting his turn to bat. Friends remember that it was easy to tell when Roberto was up. He always stayed up the longest. It seemed as if he could hit the ball anywhere it was pitched.

Life in Puerto Rico was not all fun. Roberto's father, Melchor Clemente, was a sugarcane cutter. Puerto Rico's main industry was sugarcane, which is used to make sugar as well as rum. Puerto Rico is known around the world for its rum. The island was filled with large sugarcane fields that had to be harvested by hand. Workers

A group of workers harvest sugarcane. The stalks are cut at ground level and bundled whole for transport to a mill.

During the hard times of the Great Depression, many Puerto Rican families could not afford good housing. They lived in slums, such as the one above.

toiled in ninety-degree heat while swinging long knives, called machetes, to cut the long sugarcane stalks. They worked only a few feet from other workers using machetes. It was not unusual for men to be cut, injured, or even killed as a result of accidents caused by the swinging blades. The stalks were also very sharp, so the men had to wear long-sleeved shirts, which made them even more uncomfortable in the heat.

Roberto was born in the town of Carolina on August 18, 1934, during the Great Depression, a time of failing businesses and extreme economic hardship for many people. Most families could not afford many luxuries.

Roberto Clemente's homeland, Puerto Rico, is a small island in the Caribbean Sea. It lies just southeast of the U.S. mainland, 1,000 miles off the coast of Florida. The island is not big—about the size of the state of Rhode Island—but over the decades, it has had a big impact on baseball in the United States. Apart from Clemente, the island has produced baseball stars such as Juan Gonzalez, Roberto Alomar, Ivan Rodriguez, and Bernie Williams.

Puerto Rico may seem exotic to many Americans, with its sandy beaches, tropical climate, and Spanish-speaking locals. But Puerto Rico is not a foreign country. It is a part of the United States. Specifically, it is a commonwealth territory belonging to the United States. As a commonwealth, it receives assistance and protection from the United States, and its inhabitants are U.S. citizens. They can come to the mainland without immigration restrictions. Puerto Ricans elect their own governor but cannot vote in U.S. presidential elections.

The first inhabitants of Puerto Rico were the Arawak Indians. In 1493 Christopher Columbus landed there and claimed it for Spain. Fifteen years later, Spanish and other European settlers began to arrive and colonize (settle) the island. They killed or enslaved most of the Indians. Other Indians died of diseases that the Europeans brought, for which the Indians had no cure. Many Indians intermarried with Spanish settlers, and their descendants still live in Puerto Rico. However, no full-blooded Indians are known to live there any longer. Beginning in 1510, black people were brought to the island from Africa as slaves. Like the Indians, many slaves intermarried with the Spanish. Their descendents are black Latinos, who also still live in Puerto Rico. Most of the island's modern population is of Spanish descent.

While Spain ruled Puerto Rico, the Spanish built large forts and impressive cities on the island. Puerto Rico, which means "rich port" in Spanish, originally referred only to the port city that is now its capital city, San Juan. It became an important port for Spanish merchants as well as for black-market smugglers. In 1873 Spain ended slavery in Puerto Rico and the island was taken over by the United States after the Spanish-American War in 1898.

Modern Puerto Rico continues to be one of the great shipping destinations in the world, especially San Juan. One of its greatest products, apart from baseball players, is rum made from sugarcane. The world-famous Bacardi rum is made here and shipped all over the world. The island is also becoming a source of high-tech and medical products. It has its own Olympics team and competes in the games as an independent nation.

The Clementes did not have indoor plumbing. Dinner usually consisted of rice and beans. But Melchor made sure enough rice and beans were always on the table for Roberto and his seven older brothers and sisters to eat. And the family was always loving and supportive. They often would gather in the evenings and talk, telling stories and jokes.

The hard times meant that Melchor had to work extra jobs to earn additional money for the family. He ran a small store where he sold things to other workers. He also owned a truck that he hired out to people for deliveries. The Clemente boys would help out by loading and unloading the truck. Their mother, Luisa Walker Clemente, also had a job, washing clothes for the family that owned the plantation (large farm) where her husband worked. Luisa was a dignified, cheerful woman. She brought Roberto to church regularly, where he learned strong values. Roberto's parents always made sure that he treated everyone with respect.

Melchor thought it was especially important to teach his son about hard work, responsibility, and growing up. One day Melchor took his son to work with him. While they were both standing by the side of a dirt road, the boss came driving by in a shining automobile. The car kicked up a lot of dirt into the faces of the workers, including Roberto and his father. Melchor pointed to the boss and told his son to always remember that having money did not make a man better than other people.

When Roberto was nine, some of his friends owned bicycles, and he wanted one too. At that time, most everyone in Carolina rode horses, mules, or bicycles because no one could afford a car. Even owning a bicycle was a very big deal. Getting a bicycle would mark an important part of Roberto's childhood. Melchor considered his son's request and then said yes.

Roberto could hardly believe his ears. But Melchor then added that Roberto could have the bicycle only if he could pay for it himself. Roberto was deflated at first, but he rose to the challenge. For almost three years, he ran errands and carried heavy milk cans for neighbors. He would often have to get up at six in the morning to go get the milk, but he stuck with it until he earned the twenty-seven dollars he needed.

When he got older, Roberto went to work with his father in the sugarcane fields. He liked this work because it made him feel equal with his older brothers, who also worked in the fields. But Roberto's parents did not want him to follow in his father's footsteps. They didn't think he should be a baseball player, either, though that is what Roberto dreamed of being. The family thought Roberto would be better off spending his time going to school and studying. His mother wanted him to become an engineer and build beautiful things. But no matter what they said, Roberto was convinced that he was going to be a baseball player.

It took time for Luisa to come around to the idea. She would often get upset when her son came home with his best clothes filthy from playing in the dirt field. Sometimes she would send Roberto on an errand, and he would be gone for hours because he came across a baseball game and joined in. During the summer, he would get up in the morning, leave, and not come back again until dinnertime. Roberto was often late for dinner or missed dinner entirely because he lost track of time playing ball. "I would forget to eat because of baseball," Clemente later recalled.

One time the boy came home carrying his most treasured possession, his baseball bat. He was late for dinner as usual, and he could tell his mom was angry. She asked him where he had been, and he admitted he had been playing baseball. To teach him a lesson, she took the bat and went to the fireplace. She started a fire, then tossed her boy's bat into it. The boy was horrified and quickly grabbed the scorched bat out of the fire. But he learned his lesson. He promised his parents he would never be late again. He kept his promise.

When Roberto wasn't playing baseball, he was listening to baseball games on the radio. He especially liked to listen to games from the Puerto Rican Winter League. Many major-league players came to Puerto Rico to play when the big-league season in the United States was over. Among those who played in Puerto Rico was Monte Irvin, a New York Giants outfielder with a powerful throwing arm. Roberto liked Irvin so much and talked about him so often that Roberto's friends nicknamed him Monte.

Some Saturdays Melchor gave Roberto twenty-five cents—ten cents to ride the bus into nearby San Juan and fifteen cents for a ticket into Sixto Escobar Stadium, where the San Juan Senators played. Roberto eventually

When he was in high school, Monte Irvin *(right)* set a record for throwing the javelin at his New Jersey school. Roberto also excelled in throwing the javelin when he reached high school.

found the courage to ask his hero Irvin for an autograph, and the two soon became friends. Roberto would carry Irvin's glove for him, and Irvin often gave him baseballs.

Roberto was so devoted to becoming a better baseball player that he always carried a small rubber ball. He would squeeze the ball in his hands to build up his strength. And he would bounce the ball on the floor, against a wall, or even against a ceiling so he could improve his catching ability. He bounced the ball so that he could imagine catching fly balls, line drives, and grounders.

Roberto drove the whole family crazy with his rubber ball, which could be heard all over the house and at all hours of the day and night. Sleeping was difficult for everyone because Roberto would bounce balls against the walls and ceiling in his room when he should have been sleeping. But as he got older, all the practice finally started to pay off. People outside the family began to notice his ability to play ball.

chapter 2

TURNING HEADS, TURNING PRO

One afternoon in a field in Carolina, fourteen-year-old Roberto Clemente was playing baseball with his friends. Their game, played as usual with sticks and tin cans and old coffee sacks, caught the attention of Roberto Marin. Marin was a part-time high school teacher and a rice salesman for the Sello Rojo rice company. He was also the manager of a slow-pitch softball team sponsored by Sello Rojo. He often drove around the neighborhoods of Carolina and San Juan looking for players for his team.

Watching Clemente swat tin cans all over the field, Marin could tell he had a special talent. He asked the young man to try out for his team. Clemente made the team and was given his first baseball uniform: a red and white T-shirt with the Sello Rojo team logo on it.

Clemente played shortstop for Sello Rojo because the team needed infield help. He often made spectacular stops of ground balls and even more spectacular, cannon-like throws across the infield. After two years, Marin switched his team to a fast-pitch league. He also switched Clemente to the outfield to take advantage of his great arm. Clemente practiced hard to become a good out-fielder. He regularly made one or two great catches a game, often while diving to the ground or running into a fence. Clemente had trouble hitting the faster-moving softballs, but he continued to practice hard. He began to develop more muscle, especially in his arms and hands, because he still walked around constantly squeezing a rubber ball. He worked all the time to become a better ballplayer.

Before long, other teams on the island noticed Clemente. By the time Clemente was sixteen, he had several teams chasing after him. He joined a well-known Double-A amateur baseball team called Juncos. With Juncos, Clemente had to adjust to hitting baseballs, which were pitched overhand. They are pitched much harder than fast-pitched softballs, which are pitched underhand. Out of a sense of loyalty, he also continued to play softball for Sello Rojo.

Clemente attended high school at Julio Vizcarrondo High School in Carolina. He was not a great student, but his teachers recalled that he was soft-spoken and respectful at all times. He played on the school baseball team as a shortstop. He was a standout player on the team, but he was better known for his abilities on the track-and-field team.

Clemente became so good at track and field that many people thought he would represent Puerto Rico in the 1952 Olympic Games in Helsinki, Finland. Clemente was good at the triple jump and the high jump. He was also

Athletes compete in the track-and-field events at the 1952 Olympic Games in Finland.

incredibly fast. In one meet, he ran the 440-yard race and beat not only the best man on his team but also the fastest 440-yard runner on the whole island.

Clemente's best event was the javelin, which required a combination of speed and power to throw a long metal stick. At one point, Clemente threw the javelin 195 feet, considered incredible for a high school athlete. Although going to the Olympics was tempting, Clemente was within sight of his dream of becoming a professional baseball player. He decided to focus all of his energy on the sport he loved.

Roberto Marin, who had become a good friend and mentor to Clemente, thought the boy was ready to move up to a higher league and contacted the owner of the Santurce Crabbers, Pedro Zorilla. The Santurce Crabbers was one of the many professional minor-league teams that played around San Juan all year. Zorilla was known as Mr. Baseball in Puerto Rico and had many connections with major league teams. Zorilla did some scouting for the Brooklyn Dodgers and arranged for Clemente to try out for that U.S. team.

In the 1950s, the Dodgers were one of the most famous teams in baseball. They were famous partly because they were successful, but also because of what they did in 1947. That year the Dodgers made history by breaking baseball's so-called color barrier, the unofficial rule that banned African Americans from playing Major League Baseball. In 1947 the Dodgers took the bold step of signing Jackie Robinson to be the first African American man to play in the big leagues.

Branch Rickey *(right)* welcomes Jackie Robinson *(left)* to the Brooklyn Dodgers. The first year was tough for Robinson as the league's only African American player. But his skill on the diamond earned him the Rookie of the Year award.

The Dodgers also proved to be pioneers in signing Latin American players. Although Latino players were allowed to play in the big leagues, not many of them had done so over the years. The Dodgers knew that Puerto Rico and other Caribbean lands had a lot of talented players. To find the top players, they hired Al Campanis as their main Latin American scout.

Campanis spent his time in Puerto Rico and other places looking for ballplayers. Apart from attending hundreds of games each year, Campanis and other scouts also held public tryouts. The tryouts provided an opportunity for any player to show what he could do on a diamond. It

Al Campanis *(left)* played a few games for the Brooklyn Dodgers before joining the U.S. Navy during World War II (1939–1945). When he returned from the war, he became a manager and worked for the Dodgers for forty-six years.

was not unusual for hundreds of boys to show up on try-out day, but the scouts knew it was likely none of them would be good enough to play in the big leagues. Still, there was always the chance that one would prove good enough.

On the day that Clemente tried out, seventy-one other players tried out with him. Clemente's abilities made him stand out right away. While every other player at the try-out floated the ball softly to home, Clemente's throws from the outfield to the catcher were bullets. They would pop loudly into the catcher's glove. Campanis was immediately impressed.

Campanis grew even more impressed when he saw how fast Clemente could run. The young players were asked to run 60 yards, and Clemente easily outran all the others. In fact, Clemente ran so fast in the 60-yard dash—in 6.4 seconds—that he was within 0.3 seconds of the world record for that event. And he did it despite wearing a baggy baseball uniform, clunky baseball cleats, and running on soft grass. The time was so incredible that Campanis asked Clemente to run it again, just to make sure the watch was working. It was. Clemente again registered 6.4 seconds.

Campanis sent all the other players home. Roberto Clemente was the only player he wanted to watch. While he was optimistic about the young prospect based on his arm and speed, the big test would be whether the seventeen-year-old could hit. When Clemente slammed line drive after line drive off of the outfield fences—and ten balls over the fence—Campanis had seen enough. Even when the pitcher threw balls way outside the strike zone, Clemente was able to reach them and stroke them into the outfield.

Campanis wanted to sign him right then, but there was a problem. Clemente was still in high school and not yet eighteen years old. At that time, Major League Baseball rules said that a player could not sign a contract until he was eighteen. This greatly worried Campanis because it meant that another team might discover Clemente while he and the Dodgers waited for him to come of age. He feared that the Dodgers' biggest rivals—the other New York teams, the Yankees and the Giants—might sign him.

Clemente in his Santurce Crabbers uniform

The Yankees, at that time, had Mickey Mantle in their outfield, and the Giants had Willie Mays in theirs. Campanis feared that Clemente would end up playing alongside Mays or Mantle, making the competition for the Dodgers even tougher.

In the meantime, Zorilla, who also had attended the tryout, offered Clemente a chance to play on his team. Zorilla gave Clemente his first professional baseball contract. He paid Clemente forty dollars a week to play for the Crabbers and gave him a four-hundred-dollar bonus to sign a contract. Clemente also got a brand-new glove to use in right field.

Campanis and the Dodgers were understandably nervous while they waited for Clemente to turn eighteen. They kept track of him while he played for the Crabbers. With Santurce, Clemente played with and against many big leaguers who came to Puerto Rico to take part in the winter league. He impressed them with his all-around ability.

Finally, in February of 1954, the Dodgers offered Clemente a contract. They thought so highly of Clemente that they offered him a ten-thousand-dollar bonus to sign. Most Puerto Rican players at that time received about five hundred dollars to sign a contract. Clemente quickly agreed.

Later the same day, however, the Milwaukee Braves called on Clemente and asked him to sign with them. Milwaukee was willing to pay Clemente a bonus of nearly thirty thousand dollars. Clemente could not believe it. He had agreed to play for the Dodgers, but this was so much money he couldn't decide what he should do. He finally asked his parents for advice.

His mother asked him if he had promised the Dodgers he would play for them. He said that he had. Then, she said, the decision was simple. Clemente knew she was right. He had given the Dodgers his word. On February 19, he signed a contract with the team.

chapter 3

A LONG WAY FROM HOME

When the time came to leave Puerto Rico after graduating from high school, Roberto Clemente was very excited. He was going to play baseball for the world-famous Brooklyn Dodgers! But he was also nervous. He had never been on an airplane before. He had never been away from home for such a long time. He had rarely been outside of Carolina, much less to a place as big as the United States.

His dad advised him to take care of himself. "Buy yourself a good car and don't depend on anybody," Melchor said.

Clemente was sent to the Dodgers' Triple-A team in Montreal, Canada—the Royals. The major-league team had a great outfield at that time, with Jackie Robinson and All-Stars Duke Snider and Carl Furillo. The Dodgers didn't think it was a good idea to place Clemente with the big club because he wouldn't get to play much. And if he didn't play much, he wouldn't get better. As good as Clemente was, he still had a lot to learn about being a major-league player.

But sending Clemente to Triple-A presented a problem for the Dodgers. Major League Baseball rules at the time stated that if a team paid more than four thousand dollars to sign a player, then they had to keep him on their major-league roster for the whole year. Any player who was not placed on the team's major-league roster could be snatched up by another club in a draft in the off-season.

The Dodgers pose for their 1954 team photo. Clemente was not part of the major-league club and was sent to the minor leagues instead.

The rule was designed to keep rich teams from stockpiling all the best players.

The Dodgers sent Clemente to the minor leagues anyway, knowing they were taking a chance on losing him. But the club had a plan to hide him. Montreal was far from the major-league cities in the United States. They hoped few scouts would make it up there. Also, the Montreal manager, Max Macon, was under strict instructions to put Clemente on the bench when he was playing well. This way the other teams would not see how good he was.

In a game during the first week of the season, Clemente blasted a four-hundred-foot home run to left field, into a strong wind, that flew all the way out of the stadium. It was an impressive feat. Few Montreal players had the power to clear the fence in left field, much less the entire building. But the next day, Clemente found himself on the bench. In another game, Clemente was due to bat with the bases loaded, a great opportunity to knock in some runs. But the manager sent someone to pinch-hit for him (sent another player to bat instead). In another game, he hit three triples, only to find himself benched again the next day.

Clemente grew discouraged. He did not understand why the Dodgers would pay him five thousand dollars a year if they were not going to give him a chance to play. He complained to Macon but was told that it was for his own good. That only confused Clemente. Some of the older players on the team, most of whom had been playing in the Dodgers organization for a number of years, knew what was going on. They tried to explain to the young man what was happening, but that didn't make Clemente feel better either.

Making matters worse was the fact that Montreal was so different from Clemente's Puerto Rico. The city was thousands of miles away from the island, and it was cold much of the year. Even in the summer, snow lingered on the Canadian mountains. And Clemente spoke mainly Spanish. Most of the people in Montreal spoke French or English. Clemente knew little English and no French at all. Such simple things as riding a bus to and from the stadium or even eating dinner out at a restaurant became difficult because of the language barrier.

Things got worse. When the team played in the United States, especially in the South, Clemente had to deal with racism and segregation. Segregation was a law enforced at that time that kept African Americans and white people separate. They had to use separate bathrooms and drinking fountains, sit in different sections on buses, eat in separate restaurants, and sleep in separate hotels. Like many Puerto Ricans, Clemente was a black Latino. In the United States, he was treated like a black man. He, like other black players, was not allowed to stay or eat at the same hotels as their white teammates. Black players were often harassed and insulted by white fans.

Remembering the lessons that his father had taught him, Clemente learned to deal with such problems. He recalled how his father had told him early in life to work hard, be a good man, and be a serious person. As

In most parts of the South in the 1950s, bus terminal waiting rooms were segregated.

a result, Clemente carried himself with dignity. He always dressed in a suit. He always treated people with respect, even when faced with prejudice in stores, restaurants, or hotels.

The lack of playing time and the other difficulties wore on Clemente. He missed his family. Having to go through so many frustrating experiences alone made him wonder if he had made a mistake in signing with the Dodgers.

"I want to go home, Mr. Campanis," Clemente said one day to the man who had discovered him. "I know I can play better than these guys, but they won't let me play."

Campanis told the young man to relax and be patient, but things got even worse. The Dodgers barely played Clemente over the final twenty-five games of the season. Perhaps their plan to hide the budding star would have worked, except for two problems. First, Clemente was too good. When he did get in games, he played so well that other major-league teams couldn't help but notice. The second problem was Branch Rickey.

For years Rickey had been one of the Dodgers' best talent spotters. He was famous for being the man who had signed Jackie Robinson for the Dodgers. Before that, Rickey had helped put together the Saint Louis Cardinals teams of the 1930s, some of the best teams ever to play.

Branch Rickey (right) not only had an eye for good talent, but he was responsible for several improvements to the Major League Baseball system as well. These improvements include the modern farm system for developing players and the use of statistics to track performance.

But by 1954, the Dodgers had lost Rickey to the rival Pittsburgh Pirates. Rickey was hard at work trying to fix his new team—one of the worst teams in the league. Rickey saw Clemente play, and he knew right away that he had to have him for his Pirates.

So at the end of the 1954 season, the Pirates drafted and signed Clemente away from the Dodgers. The team wanted him, even though Clemente hadn't played much in Montreal and had only a .257 batting average. (Batting average is a percentage of hits a player gets per times at bat. A .257 average means Clemente got a hit 25.7 percent of the time—not a very impressive average.) Although Clemente had wanted to play for the Dodgers, he was happy to be going to an organization that wanted him. Clemente had no doubts about his ability, but he did have one concern: where was Pittsburgh?

He didn't know, and he didn't really care. Clemente, at the age of twenty, was finally on his way to the major leagues.

Clemente was excited to finally join the major leagues for the 1955 season.

chapter 4

THE MAN OF STEEL

In the winter of 1954–1955, after signing with the Pirates, Clemente went home to Puerto Rico. He played winter ball with the Santurce Crabbers, which also had Willie Mays and the talented veteran Bob Thurman in its outfield that year. Clemente had a great season for Santurce. Led by its hard-hitting, slick-fielding outfield, the Crabbers also had a great season. They won the Puerto Rican Winter League title and went on to win the Caribbean World Series.

But the winter also brought misfortune to Clemente and his family. His brother Luis was found to have a brain tumor, which doctors said was untreatable. During his stay in Puerto Rico, Clemente visited his brother often. One evening, as Clemente was on his way home from the hospital, he got into a car accident.

His car was hit by a drunk driver who had run a red light going sixty miles per hour. The accident severely injured Clemente's back, which would give him pain for the rest of his career. Luis died a short time later, on New Year's Eve.

When spring rolled around, Clemente was ready to join his new team—which needed his help. Pittsburgh had an awful baseball team in the 1950s. The Pirates had finished dead last for three straight years when Clemente arrived. It had been more than thirty years since the Pirates had won a World Series championship.

Almost as soon as Clemente arrived in Fort Myers, Florida, for spring training, he was again exposed to the racism he had encountered the previous year in the American South. A newspaper writer wrote that a "Puerto Rican hot dog" had arrived in town. *Hot dog* is a negative term for a show-off. Clemente was irritated that the writer had unfairly stereotyped him, even though the writer had never seen him play (or show off). But he didn't let it affect his playing.

Baseball managers often use spring training to evaluate their players and decide which ones will be their everyday players. With the Pirates having struggled so much in recent years, many positions were up for grabs in 1955. Clemente, however, did not earn a role as a starting outfielder out of spring training, even though he had hit for a .395 average. During the first three games of the regular season, he found himself sitting on the Pittsburgh bench, watching another player in right field. The Pirates lost all three games.

A few Pirates show off their knuckle ball technique during spring training in the mid-1950s.

Then, on April 17, during the team's first home game of the year, Pittsburgh manager Fred Haney made a lineup change. He put Roberto Clemente in right field and batting third. At age twenty, Clemente was a starting Major League Baseball player.

The game was against Clemente's old team, the Brooklyn Dodgers. In his first major-league at bat, Clemente smashed a hard bouncer toward the Brooklyn shortstop, Pee Wee Reese. As Reese knocked down the ball, Clemente ran hard and beat the throw to first base. With the single, Clemente was one-for-one in his big-league

Pee Wee Reese was an outstanding shortstop and captain. He played sixteen seasons with the Dodgers, leading them to seven World Series.

career. The next batter hit a triple, scoring Clemente, but the Pirates lost again, 10–3.

Clemente had played well enough to get the start in another game that same afternoon, the second in a doubleheader against Brooklyn. He got two more hits, but the Pirates lost again, 3–2. Clemente played the next game too when the Pirates traveled to New York to play the Giants. Clemente's former Santurce teammate, Willie Mays, played for the Giants, as did his boyhood hero Monte Irvin. Before the game, Clemente spoke with both players and got some hitting advice from Mays. Perhaps inspired, he got two hits that game, including an inside-the-park home run. He also gunned down a base runner from the outfield, showing

Willie Mays *(right)* was an exceptional ball player. Over his career, he accumulated 3,283 hits and 660 home runs.

off his powerful throwing arm. Again, however, the Pirates lost, 12–3.

It was probably too much to expect that just one young man from Puerto Rico would turn things around for the struggling Pirates. He was still a rookie, and despite his natural ability, he was still a raw talent. The Pirates lost their first eight games before earning a win. They finished the season with only sixty wins in 154 games—which at least was seven more wins than the previous season—and in last place for the fourth straight year. And although Clemente had started with a hot bat, he cooled down as the season progressed. He played in 124 games in 1955, got up to bat almost five hundred times, and ended up hitting .255 for the season. He also broke dozens of plastic batting helmets, by smashing them with a bat when he had poor at bats.

Yet Clemente consistently shone in the outfield. He was an outstanding defensive player, making thrilling catches by jumping up against the walls or diving to the ground. He made rocketlike throws, putting out many base runners who dared test his arm. It didn't take long for his passionate and exciting play to earn him great popularity among fans in Pittsburgh. Adding

Clemente always gave his best while on the field. He never hesitated to jump against the walls to make a great catch.

Excited by Clemente's passion for the game, young fans flocked to him for autographs. Clemente always had time for his fans, which earned him even greater appreciation.

to the fans' appreciation of him was that he spent hours signing autographs and chatting with fans before and after games.

In spite of his popularity with some fans, Clemente was having trouble adjusting to life in the United States. He still did not speak English very well, and a lot of the food and customs were still very strange to him. He struggled throughout the season to speak properly and be understood. Many people in Pittsburgh, even teammates and his manager, made fun of the way Clemente talked. Some of his teammates even used racial slurs in talking about him. Many fans sent him letters calling him racist names and telling him to return home to the "jungle."

Clemente had an especially hard time with newspaper writers. Many sportswriters stereotyped him in their stories and made fun of his heavily accented speech. They often quoted him phonetically, such as printing "veree" for very and "gut" for good. The stories made Clemente look ignorant and illiterate. He quickly developed a frosty relationship with the press.

Pittsburgh, which was known as the Steel City because of its steel mills, was mainly a white city. As a black

The bustling city of Pittsburgh was overwhelming at first for Clemente.

Latino, Clemente often felt alone and frustrated in this foreign city, but he soon found a friend. A Pirate teammate introduced him to a postal employee named Phil Dorsey, and the two hit it off right away. Dorsey was also black and provided Clemente with a much-needed confidant and companion. With help from Dorsey, Clemente became more comfortable living in Pittsburgh and speaking English.

For the 1956 season, the Pirates hired a new manager, Bobby Bragan, who immediately put his hitting coach to work on improving Clemente's batting. Part of the reason Clemente's bat cooled off as the previous season had gone on was that opposing pitchers had learned that he would swing at almost any pitch, even ones way out of the strike zone. So they very rarely threw him good pitches to hit. Another reason for his slide was that he didn't hold his head steady, and so sometimes he couldn't keep his eye on the ball. The hitting coach, George Sisler, and Clemente worked hard to improve his pitch selection and his form.

The work paid off in 1956. For much of the season, Clemente was among the league leaders in batting, and as late as June, his Pirates were holding onto first place. The team had dropped most of its older veterans and replaced them with younger players to form an inexperienced but exciting team. But the Pirates faded at the end of the season, finishing in seventh place, second to last in the National League. Clemente finished with a .311 average—a big improvement over 1955's average.

Clemente celebrates with teammates after winning a game in 1956. *From left to right*: Clemente, Dale Long, Ron Kline, and Frank Thomas.

Clemente and his team suffered a setback in 1957. His back injury gave him great pain all year long, and he endured several other injuries. He missed forty-three games and finished with an unimpressive .253 batting average. The Pirates finished tied for last place.

Over the next couple years, though the Pirates continued to struggle, Clemente improved and showed that he had the makings of a star. And each year, the fans fell more in love with him and his all-out playing style. He chased down fly balls in the outfield with relentless concentration, often unleashing the "Clemente cannon" to throw out base runners. At the plate, he did it all—scalded line drives and homers, bunted for base hits, and ran out every ground ball. He chugged around the bases with a zeal that was often reckless. When he stepped into the batter's box, the crowd roared.

But Clemente's relationship with the press got worse. Some sportswriters criticized him for complaining too much about injuries. Each time Clemente came to bat, he would take a long time to get in the batter's box. He had an elaborate routine for stretching his shoulders, his arms, and his aching back. Because Clemente ran around the bases so fast, the writers could not believe that Clemente could be hurt.

Clemente's back continued to cause him problems, despite his elaborate routine for stretching when at bat.

>MY FOOT WAS SORE

Despite the bumps and bruises Clemente suffered, he was in the lineup almost every day. During one game early in his career, Clemente complained about having a sore foot. He got on base, and the next batter got a hit. Clemente flew around the bases and scored all the way from first on the single. Someone asked him how he was able to run so fast if he was hurt. "My foot was sore," he said. "I ran all the way home so I could rest it on the bench."

Clemente slides into base. He never let his many injuries get in the way of playing a good game.

Off the field, Clemente had to work on his bad back constantly. He eventually was so good at treating his back that he became an expert on the subject. In fact, during the off-season, people in Puerto Rico often came to his house to seek treatment for their backs. It did not matter what time of day or night it was, Clemente never turned them away.

Clemente knew he owed his success to his hard work, but he also was extremely superstitious. If he was playing well or if the Pirates were winning, he would not change anything because he did not want to break the lucky streak. One time the Pirates won eleven games in a row, and Clemente did not change his clothes during that whole time. In this way, Clemente was like many professional athletes, who will do just about anything to keep a lucky streak alive.

By the end of the decade, the Pirates had become more than respectable. And Clemente had become very good, but not yet great. The 1960 season was a breakthrough year for him and his team. Clemente had a strong season batting, finishing the year with a .314 average, his career high so far. He also had career highs of 16 home runs and 94 runs batted in. And on the last game of the year, the Pirates clinched the National League pennant. They were on their way to the World Series for the first time since 1927.

The World Series is the biggest stage upon which a professional baseball player performs. The Series, as it is sometimes called, matches the champions of the American and the National leagues. It is played at the end of each season, usually in October, which gave rise to its nickname of the fall classic.

Roger Maris *(left)* and Mickey Mantle *(right)* were among the best hitters in baseball when the Pirates faced off against them in the 1960 World Series.

In 1960 the Pirates faced the American League champion New York Yankees. Their powerhouse lineup included the great sluggers Mickey Mantle and Roger Maris. New York was heavily favored to win. But Pittsburgh had better pitching, and the Pirates won the first game of the best-of-seven series by shutting down the Yankee hitters. The Yankees bounced back and took games two and three, and the Pirates again pitched well enough to win game four. The two teams split the next two games, which left game seven to determine the world champions.

Game seven was played in Pittsburgh. Pirates pitchers couldn't keep the Yankee hitters in check this time, and in the eighth inning, New York led 7–4. Things did not look good for the Pirates. But the team exploded for five runs in the bottom of the eighth to take the lead, 9–7, only to see New York tie it in the top of the ninth.

Pirates second baseman Bill Mazeroski led off the bottom of the ninth against Yankee pitcher Ralph Terry. Mazeroski swung at the second pitch Terry threw and yanked it into the seats for a home run. The crowd exploded in joy. The Pirates were world champions.

Bill Mazeroski is rushed by fans as he nears home on his ninth-inning home run to clinch the 1960 World Series for the Pirates.

After the game, while the Pittsburgh players celebrated wildly in the clubhouse, Clemente quietly slipped away. He later said that he had gone off to walk the streets of Pittsburgh where fans were still celebrating. Clemente always considered himself a man of the people, and he thought he should be among them at this moment.

chapter 5

THE GREAT ONE

The 1960 season and World Series established Clemente as one of the best players in the game. He had had the best season of his career and hit safely in every game of the World Series. After the season, Clemente's teammate Dick Groat won the National League Most Valuable Player (MVP) award. Clemente congratulated Groat, but he thought he had had a better year than his teammate. He believed he had not won the prestigious award because he was Latino. He promised to do even better the following year.

Clemente lived up to his promise. In 1961 he batted .351, which was better than anyone else in the National League—the first time in Clemente's career he had won the batting title and the first time a Puerto Rican had won it. He won his first Gold Glove award as the best fielder at his position. He made the All-Star Game and drove in the winning run in the game. He did not win the MVP that year either, though. Yet thousands of people greeted him at the airport when he arrived in San Juan after the season. He had become a hero to the people of Puerto Rico.

After the 1963 season, Clemente went home to Puerto Rico as usual. One day that winter, he saw a beautiful woman at the pharmacy where he was filling a prescription. He talked to her briefly, then went home and told his mother that he had just met the woman he was going to

Clemente poses with fellow All-Stars Willie Mays *(center)* and Hank Aaron *(right)*.

Clemente knew he wanted to marry Vera the minute he saw her. They were wed in his hometown of Carolina, Puerto Rico.

marry. The woman's name was Vera Cristina Zabala, and it was not long before the two had their first date. They attended a baseball game in San Juan. The two hit it off and continued to see each other. They were married the following off-season, on November 14, 1964, when Clemente was thirty years old. The couple had a son almost right away, Roberto Jr. In the next couple years, they had two more sons, Luis and Enrique.

Also during the 1964–1965 off-season, Clemente organized and hosted several baseball clinics for underprivileged kids in Puerto Rico. He had long wanted to create a sports center for kids—a place where kids could go for free to play and learn about sports. It was just one of many things Clemente did for others, especially those who were needy. Since he had become a star, he wanted to use his celebrity for good causes.

Clemente met the great humanitarian and civil rights pioneer Martin Luther King Jr when King was in Puerto Rico in 1964. The two became friends. Like King, Clemente spoke out about racism. Conditions of racism had improved since he first came to the United States in 1955. Civil rights laws guaranteeing equal rights for American citizens of all races had been passed. Yet discrimination continued in the United States. Clemente and other minority players were often not treated fairly on or off the field.

Clemente helped other, younger Latino baseball players adjust to life in the big leagues. He often counseled these players, who did not speak English or know U.S. customs very well. He spoke publicly about the rights and challenges of Latino baseball players. For example, many scouts and coaches complained about Latinos who played well in their home countries but would not play well when they came to the United States. Clemente explained how hard the adjustment was for Latinos—the language barrier and the racism were hard to get used to. He advised the scouts to be patient with young Latinos. "It takes time for us to settle down emotionally," he said. "Once we're at peace with the world, we can do the job." In many ways, he was like Jackie Robinson, a good example for Latino players in the way Robinson had been for African American players.

Clemente also bought his parents a house and took in young relatives whose parents had died. And he frequently visited sick children in hospitals around Pittsburgh. He patiently signed autographs for fans, even if he was there for a very long time. One time a little girl in a wheelchair waited hours to get Clemente's autograph. She and her mother missed their bus home, so Clemente drove them home. After all, he liked to say, it was the fans who paid his salary. He felt proud when kids asked for his autograph.

Though Clemente's fan base continued to grow, the star never lost the patience to sign autographs for all of his adoring fans.

>A NEAR MUGGING

Though he was a star for the Pittsburgh Pirates, Clemente was respected by baseball fans all over the United States. One night in Saint Louis, Missouri, he went out walking to look for dinner. He bought a bag of fried chicken to take back to his hotel room. Then, as he walked, a car pulled up next to him and thugs put a gun in his face.

The robbers forced him into the car and made him take off his clothes. They stole his wallet and even his bag of chicken. But when they looked in his wallet and saw his identification, they realized who he was. Then their attitude changed completely. They apologized to Clemente and gave him his clothes and wallet back. They then let him out and drove off.

Suddenly, Clemente saw the car turn around and come back to where he was standing on the sidewalk. He thought they had changed their minds and were coming back to kill him. Instead, when the car pulled up, the robbers threw his bag of chicken back to him.

Clemente was well liked by his teammates. Here he shares a joke with teammate Fred Green.

By the 1960s, Clemente had become the leader of the Pittsburgh clubhouse. He would joke with players to keep them from getting tense before big games and play cards with them during trips to pass the time. Always, he would lead by example, practicing for hours and playing as hard as he could during games.

Clemente was one of the most serious players in the game, and on his off days, he was just as serious. He spent much of his time alone. Instead of reading the sports pages, Clemente read novels—westerns and adventure books. One of his favorite hobbies was making things out of clay. He made a lot of pieces, which he used as lamps for his home. He also taught himself to play a keyboard, and on occasion he would sing for the other players.

Even in the off-season, Clemente kept himself in tremendous shape, which helped prolong his career. One ritual he felt kept him strong was drinking a special juice he invented himself—a mixture of grape juice and raw eggs. The drink not only gave him a lot of vitamins, but also a lot of protein. He also would make shakes out of ice cream, fruit, and milk.

Clemente usually got a deep massage before playing, which helped keep his body loose for the game. And if that didn't work, all he had to do was remember that playing baseball was easy compared to the life he would have had cutting sugarcane in Puerto Rico.

All the conditioning paid off in 1966. The new Pirates manager, Harry Walker, asked Clemente to hit at least 25 home runs and drive in at least 115 runs. He said that the team needed him to improve his power numbers to help it win more games. Clemente took the request seriously. Even though the Pirates' home park, Forbes Field, was the biggest in baseball, Clemente knocked homers out at a tremendous pace. That year he hit a career high 29 home runs. He also batted .317 and drove in 119 runs. The Pirates finished third and missed the playoffs, but Clemente had forced the fans and sportswriters who had criticized him to acknowledge his greatness. He was rewarded by winning the league's Most Valuable Player award at last, just beating out the Dodgers pitcher Sandy Koufax.

Forbes Field in Pittsburgh was first opened in 1909. Baseball legend Babe Ruth hit the last three home runs of his career there in 1935.

Walker held his star player in high regard. He told a magazine reporter that Clemente "is just the best player in baseball, that's all." Around Pittsburgh, Clemente was known as the Great One.

That off-season was eventful for Clemente. In November he and his family suffered the loss of another of Clemente's brothers, this one to spinal cancer. In January Clemente received a new contract from the Pirates. It paid him more than $100,000. He was one of only a few players in the major leagues who was paid so much to play. In the 1967 season, he showed he was worth it. He batted .357, with 23 homers and 110 runs batted in.

Even at the relatively old age (for a professional athlete) of thirty-six, Clemente continued to astound his managers and fans by batting for average and power. By 1970 he was well on his way to the benchmark 3,000 hits.

In 1970 the Pittsburgh Pirates made a change. The team played the first half of the season in the sixty-one-year-old Forbes Field. Halfway through the season, the team opened a new ballpark—Three Rivers Stadium—and began playing its home games there. A week after the park opened, the Pirates celebrated their new stadium and their best player by holding Roberto Clemente Night.

Fans gave Clemente a standing ovation as he walked from the dugout to the field for the ceremony. Vera and their three boys joined him on the field. Clemente's parents, along with fifteen poor children from Puerto Rico, had also been flown to Pittsburgh to take part in the event. They brought with them a piece of paper on which more than 300,000 Puerto Ricans had written their names and good wishes for Clemente.

That evening Clemente was also given many gifts, including a new car. A group of Puerto Rican soldiers presented him with a plaque. The owners of the Pirates gave Clemente's three sons a trust fund to pay for their college educations. For the event, Clemente had asked fans to make donations to Pittsburgh's Children's Hospital, and at the ceremony, he was presented with the nearly six thousand dollars that had been raised. He specified that the money was to be given to disabled children whose parents could not afford to pay medical expenses.

The evening brought great happiness to Clemente. He enjoyed the night with his parents, wife, and kids. Also attending were the mayor of Clemente's hometown and other Puerto Rican officials. The festivities

Clemente takes a moment to chat with Vera and their three sons *(from left to right: Enrique, Luis, and Roberto Jr.)* during Roberto Clemente night in 1970.

were broadcast to the entire island of Puerto Rico. When Clemente spoke in Spanish to the people of Puerto Rico, he could not help but cry.

"I want to dedicate this triumph to all the mothers in Puerto Rico," he said. "I haven't the words to express my gratitude. I only ask that those who are watching this program be close to their parents, ask for their blessing and embrace . . . and those friends who are watching or listening, shake hands in the friendship that unites all Puerto Ricans."

After the ceremony, Clemente continued the celebration by getting two hits in the game and making several fantastic catches in the outfield. He cut his leg making a running catch. He was taken out of the game and given another standing ovation. The Pirates won the game against the Houston Astros, 11–0. For the rest of the year, the team stayed right in the race for the National League East Division title. (The previous year, the National and American leagues had been divided into two divisions each—the East and the West. The winners of the divisions in each league faced each other in a five-game playoff series to determine which team would be the league champion and face the other league champion in the World Series.)

The Pirates finished the year in first place, but it had been an exhausting year for Clemente and his teammates. Clemente had fought through many injuries and missed fifty-eight games. The Pirates were swept by the Cincinnati Reds in the National League playoffs and missed the World Series.

Third-base coach Frank Oceak congratulates Clemente for hitting a home run during the 1971 World Series.

chapter 6

GOOD NIGHT, CLEMENTE

Pirates management made an important trade during the 1970 off-season, bringing in more talented players. The result was a team that was better and also had a lot of fun. The 1970 team had great chemistry and steamrolled through the season. Also, on September 1, the Pirates fielded the first all-black lineup in Major League Baseball history. For Clemente, it was a proud moment.

The Pirates finished the year in first place in their division. This time they won their playoff series against the San Francisco Giants and found themselves on their way to the World Series.

By the end of 1971, Clemente was near the end of a hugely successful career. He had been awarded eleven Gold Gloves as the best fielder at his position, he'd won four batting titles, played in fourteen All-Star games, been named Most Valuable Player once, and won a World Series championship.

Clemente was among the best players of the 1960s. But he was less well known than other baseball stars of the decade, such as Willie Mays, Hank Aaron, and Sandy Koufax, because he played in the relatively small town of Pittsburgh. The Pirates weren't often on national television. The city also did not have a large population of newspaper readers, and the last time the Pirates had been in the World Series was 1960.

For the 1971 Series, Clemente was determined to do things that would be remembered forever. The other Pirates recall that Clemente seemed to be on a mission in

Already a stellar hitter, Clemente was constantly trying to improve his game. He spent many hours in the batting cage.

1971. It was almost as if he was willing himself toward baseball immortality.

By the early 1970s, the popularity of Major League Baseball was declining. Fewer and fewer fans were attending games, and even fewer were watching the games on television. Fewer fans meant less money going into the pockets of the owners.

Part of baseball's decline had to do with the growing popularity of other sports such as football and basketball. Another reason was that baseball, unlike the other sports, still played many of its championship games during the day, while kids were in school and their parents were working. Football played its championship, the Super Bowl, on Sunday, when most people had the day off. Likewise, basketball had its playoffs on weekends or at night when people were off work and able to sit in front of their television and watch.

Baseball owners decided to follow the lead and break with tradition by playing a Series game at night. It would be on prime-time television so that millions more fans could watch without having to skip school or work. Clemente knew well the significance of the 1971 Series. There would be an estimated 60 million people watching. This World Series was going to have the largest audience to ever view Major League Baseball.

But standing in the way of Clemente were the Baltimore Orioles, one of the great dynasties in the history of the game. The Orioles, the defending world champions, appeared to be even stronger in 1971 than they were the previous year. They had four pitchers that year who had won twenty games each. They featured future Hall of Famers such as third baseman Brooks Robinson, out-fielder Frank Robinson, pitcher Jim Palmer, and manager Earl Weaver. During the 1971 season, the Orioles, for the third consecutive year, had won more than one hundred games. Everyone thought they were a lock to beat the Pirates in the Series.

Brooks Robinson dives to make a catch, showing off some of the moves that earned this third baseman his place in the National Baseball Hall of Fame.

Frank Robinson was another great Orioles player. The only player to ever be named MVP in both leagues, Robinson was a strong hitter. He currently ranks fifth all time in home runs hit.

The Pirates did not get off to a good start. In the first game, the Orioles hit three home runs and defeated Pittsburgh 5–3. The pressure only increased when Pittsburgh lost the second game as well, by a score of 11–3. Clemente had gotten two hits in each of the first two games and even made a spectacular defensive play in game two. He nearly threw out a base runner at third base with what many players said was one of the greatest throws ever seen.

But the newspapers and many baseball fans across the country were already declaring the Pirates dead. Writers even speculated about whether the Orioles could win the Series in four straight games, which would be a great embarrassment for the Pirates. As the players headed back to Pittsburgh for game three, it looked to many as if the Pirates were whipped.

Clemente, however, wouldn't let that happen. On the plane home, he promised his team that they would win. He set the tone for the Pirates when, after tapping a grounder back to Orioles pitcher Mike Cuellar in game three, he ran extra hard down to first base. The play should have been an easy out for the Orioles. But the speed with which Clemente ran so surprised Cuellar that the pitcher threw the ball away and Clemente was safe, driving in the first run of the game. The Pirates were on their way. Pittsburgh won the game, 5–1.

The fourth game was historic—the first night game in World Series history. More than 50,000 fans squeezed into Three Rivers Stadium in Pittsburgh to watch the game. More than 61 million people watched the game on television that night, the largest audience ever to watch a baseball game. The NBC television network, which broadcast the game, estimated that more than half of all the television sets in the country were tuned in to watch the Pirates and the Orioles.

After falling behind by three runs in the first inning, Clemente led Pittsburgh back to tie the game. In the third inning, he hit a pitch from the Orioles pitcher over the fence in right field. Clemente ran toward first base thinking he had hit a home run, but the umpires ruled that the ball was foul.

For about five minutes, Clemente, his manager, and his coaches argued with the umpires, who would not change their decision. Clemente finally settled down and went back to the plate. He stroked a single, then added two more hits later in the game as the Pirates won 4–3 to even the Series at two games apiece.

All of a sudden, people were taking the Pirates seriously. The fifth game would be pivotal. If Baltimore won, the Orioles would return home to play one or two games and would need to win only one of them to become world champions.

Instead, Nellie Briles of the Pirates went out and pitched a great game, allowing only two hits and shutting out the Orioles 2–0. Again, Clemente got a hit.

Nellie Briles was traded to the Pirates in 1971 from the Saint Louis Cardinals. He helped the Pirates cement their win in the 1971 World Series with his great pitching.

Returning to Baltimore, the Pirates must have thought that they were dreaming. They were one game away from winning it all. But despite another hit from Clemente, a bases empty home run, the Orioles won in ten innings, 3–2. After the game, all anyone could talk about was Clemente, who again made a tremendous throw from right field to home. The throw in the bottom of the ninth inning kept the winning run from scoring. Again, some players said it was the greatest throw they had ever seen.

The stage was set for a dramatic game seven in Baltimore. Clemente could not have asked for anything better. The game was tied 0–0 in the fourth inning, with tough Orioles lefty Mike Cuellar having retired the last eleven batters he'd faced. Clemente came up to bat with two outs. With a huge television audience looking on, Cuellar threw Clemente a high curve ball on the outside part of the plate. Clemente drilled the pitch over the fence in left-center field for a home run. When Clemente ran out to play right field in the next inning, Pirates fans who had made the trip to Baltimore cheered him on.

Pirates pitcher Steve Blass, who had struggled but kept the Orioles scoreless, gained more confidence and cruised through the next few innings. The Pirates added a run in the eighth inning, making their lead 2–0. In the bottom of the eighth, the Orioles cut the lead in half on a grounder to first by Don Buford, scoring a runner from third base. But Pittsburgh's shortstop, Jackie Hernandez, made a great play to retire the next batter.

A disappointed Mike Cuellar stands on the pitching mound while Clemente rounds the bases behind him. Clemente's hit, a home run, was the first hit scored in game seven of the 1971 World Series.

Pitcher Steve Blass leaps into the air to celebrate the Pirates' win of the 1971 World Series.

The Orioles were unable to tie. In the bottom of the ninth, Blass finished off the Orioles, giving Pittsburgh its first World Series championship in eleven years.

Clemente's performance during the Series drew rave reviews. Some writers said Clemente had played a perfect Series. Not only had he batted .414, he also had gotten a hit in every game. Including the 1960 World Series, he had hit safely in every World Series game he had played in. He had also performed brilliantly in the field. Not surprisingly, Clemente was overwhelmingly selected as the Most Valuable Player of the 1971 World Series.

As he accepted the trophy for the World Series MVP, Clemente did two things to make his team and his homeland proud. He made sure to tell the millions of people who were watching or listening to the game that his performance during the fall classic was how he played the game all the time. And in Spanish, he addressed the people of Puerto Rico and his family. He thanked them for their support and asked for his parents' blessing. As the season finally came to an end, a happy and world-famous Clemente headed home to Puerto Rico, feeling on top of the world.

Roberto Clemente in 1972. At the beginning of that year, Clemente was 118 hits away from making Major League Baseball history.

c h a p t e r 7

AN IMMORTAL MOMENT

During the 1971 season, Clemente had been considering retirement. He was getting close to forty, a time when most ballplayers are already retired. Before game seven of the World Series, he told a friend that if the Pirates won, he would retire. Still, he had played well enough during the 1971 season that it seemed as if he could go on playing forever. In the celebration after the victory, Clemente talked it over with his wife. She convinced him to change his mind and play one more season.

As Clemente and the Pirates finished spring training in 1972, their goals were to defend their world championship and also help Clemente get the 118 hits he needed to reach the magic 3,000 hit mark. Only ten other major league players in history, out of all the thousands who had played the game, had ever reached that lofty mark. And

Clemente demonstrates his powerhouse swing to reporters and fans early in the 1972 season. That swing and his cool confidence at the plate often rattled the nerves of opposing pitchers.

all of them were enshrined in the National Baseball Hall of Fame in Cooperstown, New York. Clemente wanted to reach 3,000, not only for himself but also for all of the other black and Latino players who played or had ever played baseball.

The season started off well for the Pirates, but things soon fell apart. Clemente was hitting well enough that it seemed he would reach 3,000 hits easily, but he got hurt early in the season. Clemente ended up missing most of the first half of the season with a bad ankle and bruised heels.

He finally came back. But with twenty-six games to go in the season, Clemente still needed to get 25 hits to reach the 3,000 mark. Most baseball people assumed that Clemente would have to wait until the 1973 season because it would be difficult to average one hit per game.

Clemente then went on one of the best hitting streaks of his career. As the end of the season approached, Clemente was within reach of his goal. He got hit number 2,999 on the road against future Hall of Famer Steve Carlton of the Philadelphia Phillies. At Clemente's request, the Pirates took Clemente out of the lineup because he wanted to get his 3,000th hit at home in front of the Pirates fans. The

Clemente got his 2,999th hit off left-hander and Cy Young-winner Steve Carlton *(right)* of the Philadelphia Phillies. The hit, a single, came on September 28, 1972.

Righty Tom Seaver *(left)* and Roberto Clemente *(right)* in 1972. Seaver was the best right-handed pitcher in baseball at the time. With the 3,000th hit on the line, Seaver and Clemente faced off on September 29, 1972.

Pirates were fifteen games in first place and had already clinched a playoff spot by winning their division for the third year in a row. The only drama remaining in the season was when Clemente would reach 3,000. So it was an easy decision to give Clemente the chance to get his big hit in front of his home fans during a series against the New York Mets.

The first game did not go well for Clemente. He failed to get a hit against a tough New York pitching staff. Clemente then had to face Tom Seaver in the second game. At that time, Seaver was the best right-handed pitcher in baseball. Everyone knew Clemente would have a tough time getting a hit off of him.

In the first inning, Clemente hit a grounder up the middle that shot past a couple of the fielders, even going off the glove of one of them. As Clemente stood at first base, the fans started cheering wildly because they thought his grounder was a hit. The scoreboard operators at Three Rivers Stadium thought so too, and they put up a big "H" on the scoreboard indicating a hit. (In baseball, a batted ball that a fielder misplays is called an error on the fielder. Only a clean hit that no fielder "should" catch and make an out on is called a hit.) The umpire even got the ball and gave it to Clemente at first base.

But the official scorer, who sits in the press box and decides whether something is a hit or an error, thought otherwise. He ruled the ground ball was an error on the Mets player who missed it. Soon a big "E" was flashed on the scoreboard. Clemente would have to wait for at least one

Fans crowded Pittsburgh's Three Rivers Stadium *(pictured here in 1995)*, hoping to see Clemente get his 3,000th hit on September 29, 1972. They almost got their wish, but Clemente's apparent hit was officially scored an error on the Mets' second baseman Ken Boswell.

more game to get his 3,000th because he went hitless the rest of the game. After the game, Clemente said he was glad the ground ball had been ruled an error. He said he did not want there to be any question about his 3000th hit.

The next day was the last game of the year, so the pressure was really on Clemente. It only increased when Clemente struck out in his first at bat against the Mets' Jon Matlack, who was pitching well enough that season that he was later voted the National League Rookie of the Year. Time seemed to be running out on Clemente.

The big moment finally came in the fourth inning. After getting a quick pep talk from Pirates slugger Willie Stargell, Clemente dug in and hit a line drive. The ball

With the count 0 balls and 1 strike, Clemente swings away at a curve ball from Mets' pitcher Jon Matlack. A long drive to the outfield fence, the double was Clemente's 3,000th hit.

Offering congratulations, second-base umpire Doug Harvey hands Clemente the baseball he had hit just moments before. The 3,000th hit made him one of only eleven players to reach the record and the first Latino to do so.

bounced on the outfield turf and then off the wall. The clapping had started as soon as Clemente made contact. By the time Clemente stopped at second with a double, the roar inside the stadium was deafening.

The cheering continued for what seemed like hours as the Pittsburgh fans poured out their love and affection for Clemente. For seventeen years, he had been an amazing player and an amazing humanitarian. He had carried himself with a great deal of dignity and represented the Pirates probably better than anyone in their history. The fans were saying thank you the best way they knew how.

The umpires stopped the game and handed Clemente the baseball. Clemente's old Santurce teammate, Willie Mays, who was playing for the Mets, came out to congratulate Clemente on his achievement. Clemente had done it. He was the first Latino to ever reach 3,000 hits. After the game, he dedicated the hit to Pittsburgh's fans, the people of Puerto Rico, and Roberto Marin, the man who had first given Clemente a chance to play organized baseball.

The Pirates went into the playoffs again, this time to try to repeat their world championship win. But the team did not fare well against the mighty Cincinnati Reds. The Pirates lost the playoff series three games to two. The historic season was over.

chapter 8

DEATH OF A HERO

After the 1972 season, Clemente decided not to play winter ball. He was thirty-eight years old, his back was aching, and he had more important things he wanted to do. One was to hold more baseball clinics for Puerto Rican children. Another was to do more fund-raising for the sports center he still hoped to create.

Clemente also led an amateur, all-star Puerto Rican baseball team to the Central American country of Nicaragua. The Puerto Rican all-stars played against Nicaragua's all-stars, and Clemente made many new friends in the country. Among them was a fourteen-year-old boy who had lost both of his legs in an accident. Clemente liked the boy. When Clemente discovered that he needed $750 for a pair of artificial legs, Clemente and his teammates donated the money for the operation.

Clemente spent almost all of November with the team in Nicaragua and in December was home again with his family. Then, on the night of December 23, 1972, as Clemente was preparing to celebrate Christmas with his family, news came that would change his life. A large earthquake had hit Managua, the capital of Nicaragua,

The devastating earthquake that hit Managua in 1972 flattened most of the city's buildings. Much of the area destroyed by the earthquake has never been rebuilt.

killing more than 7,000 people and injuring 20,000. The devastation was so great that at least 250,000 people were left homeless.

The news hit Clemente hard, especially as he thought about his fourteen-year-old friend. He wondered what had happened to him. He decided to help the best way that he could. He used his name and his fame in Puerto Rico to collect money, medicine, and other supplies to send to the earthquake victims. Clemente called friends of his, including a singer and a television producer, who also wanted to help.

The three began working almost immediately. Day after day, they collected tons of food, clothing, and medicines. Clemente worked fourteen hours a day on Christmas Eve, Christmas Day, and the next day. At one point, Clemente even walked from door-to-door asking people to donate whatever they could to Nicaragua. The donations were then put on planes and flown to Managua.

But word soon reached Clemente that people in Managua were stealing some of the supplies. Instead of giving the supplies for free to people who needed them, the thieves were selling them to whomever had the money to pay. Clemente became angry when he found out. He decided that the only thing to do was to fly down to Nicaragua and deliver the next planeload of supplies himself. He hoped that his being there would prevent the thieves from striking.

People who knew Clemente were not surprised that one of the most famous athletes in the world would decide to get so involved, even if it meant missing

New Year's Eve celebrations with his family and friends. Most celebrities might donate money to a cause they care about, but Clemente felt that his time and effort were more valuable than his money. He preferred hands-on work.

"It is the least I can do," he said. "Babies are dying over there. They need those supplies."

On December 31, 1972, Clemente was ready to go. He found an old plane to fly to Nicaragua. The plane was twenty years old and had had some mechanical problems. A few weeks before, its brakes had failed and it had crashed. But Clemente was anxious to get the supplies to the people, and he insisted that the plane would fly.

A pilot was hard to find, but the owner of the plane finally said he would fly it. The plane was quickly stuffed to bursting with supplies, and Clemente decided to fly on New Year's Eve, the most sacred holiday of the year for Puerto Ricans. Even though the weather was bad and people begged him not to go, Clemente assured them that things would be all right. But the plane was delayed for several hours because mechanical problems kept popping up throughout the day.

Shortly after 9:22 P.M., after a delay of more than five hours, Clemente's plane finally took off. It experienced problems almost immediately. Investigators later speculated that the supplies inside the plane were probably not tied down properly. The weight inside the plane shifted, throwing the plane off balance. One of the engines caught fire, and the plane crashed into the Atlantic Ocean just as the pilot was trying to return to the airport in San Juan.

Police and the U.S. Coast Guard searched for hours that night. Helicopters swooped and hovered over the ocean, sweeping searchlights across the water, but no trace of Clemente and the crew were found. The next day, anyone who owned a boat near San Juan took it out to look for Clemente and the plane. The remains of the

U.S. Navy divers search for the bodies of Clemente and the plane's crew twelve days after the fatal crash. Though some personal items belonging to the victims were found, no bodies were ever recovered.

plane were finally located the next day but still none of the bodies. On the beach near where the crash happened, hundreds of people came to wait for word about Clemente. Among those who searched was Clemente's teammate Manny Sanguillen, who put on scuba gear and searched for days.

As New Year's Day came to an end, it became apparent that Clemente and the crew had not survived. What was supposed to be a day of celebration instead became a day of mourning on the island. A new governor was supposed to take over the government of Puerto Rico on New Year's Day. He decided to delay the ceremonies for three days out of respect for Clemente. Millions of people all over the island were stunned and saddened by the news. The Great One was gone.

Roberto Clemente's body was never recovered, although his briefcase was found a week later on the beach. Clemente was remembered at a memorial service on January 4, 1973, in Puerto Rico. It was held at the same church where Clemente and Vera had been married and where Clemente had been baptized. Among those attending were Clemente's teammates and managers.

Another memorial service was held in Pittsburgh, attended by 1,500 people. A neon sign in the city that usually advertised beer was changed so that it read, "Adios Amigo." It means "Good-bye, Friend" in Spanish. It expressed the feelings of the city of Pittsburgh.

"He had a touch of royalty about him," said Baseball Commissioner Bowie Kuhn in expressing the feelings of

Clemente's father Melchor quietly mourns his son at the memorial service in Puerto Rico.

all Major League Baseball about the death of Clemente. "He made the word 'superstar' seem inadequate. And what a wonderfully good man he was."

People honored the memory of Clemente in different ways. On March 20, 1973, baseball writers honored Clemente by voting him into the National Baseball Hall of Fame. Usually, under the rules of Major League Baseball, a player cannot be inducted into the Hall until five years after retiring. But the writers thought Clemente deserved special treatment.

>THE HALL OF FAME

The National Baseball Hall of Fame and Museum is located in the town of Cooperstown in upstate New York. The Hall of Fame, as it is most commonly known, is probably the best-known sports shrine in the world. Founded on June 12, 1939, the Hall is where the teams, players, and legends of the game are remembered, cherished, and maintained. The Hall is open just about every day of the year. Visitors can find such sacred baseball items as Babe Ruth's bat, Willie Mays's glove, Nolan Ryan's cap, and the ball Hank Aaron hit to break the career home-run record. Also there is the jersey worn by Barry Bonds when he broke Mark McGwire's single-season home-run record in 2001.

The biggest day of the year in Cooperstown is Hall of Fame Day, when the new members are inducted. In 2004 that included dominant relief pitcher Dennis Eckersley, who saved 390 games in his career and in 1992 won the American League Most Valuable Player award as well as the American League Cy Young award (given to the best pitcher in each league). Also inducted in 2004 was Paul Molitor, an outstanding batter and base runner known for performing well when the pressure is on. He was voted the World Series Most Valuable Player in 1993 for the champion Toronto Blue Jays.

After the induction ceremonies, attended by families and friends and thousands of fans, two major-league teams play a game at Doubleday Field, which is a block from the Hall of Fame. The field is located on a former cow pasture, where legend has it that baseball was first played. It is named after Abner Doubleday, who for many years was credited with inventing the game in the 1830s. But many people now doubt that Doubleday invented baseball.

The biggest attraction at the museum is the Hall of Fame Gallery, where the plaques of all of the members are displayed. The plaques detail the members' accomplishments, as well as providing the nicknames they were known by and the teams for which they played. The first floor has exhibits featuring home-run records, no-hitters, and baseball as it is played around the world.

The second floor features a tribute each year to that season's World Series champion. The second floor also has a theater for multimedia presentations. The theater is shaped like an old baseball stadium, including wooden seats, crowd noise, and an exploding scoreboard.

Just outside the theater is a display showing a chronological history of the game. The display highlights different eras and the passage of time by showing some very special events. Included are the bat Babe Ruth used in the 1932 World Series when he called (or announced before hitting) a home run, Jackie Robinson's warm-up jacket, and the bat Roberto Clemente used to record his 3,000th (and last) hit in 1972.

Vera Clemente holds her husband's last Gold Glove award. The Pirates gave Vera the award after they retired Clemente's number.

The Pirates honored Clemente too. On April 5, 1973, they retired Clemente's number 21 so no Pirate would ever wear it again. They gave Vera Clemente a uniform jersey before the first game of the season. That year the Pirates all wore small patches with a black number 21 on their uniforms in honor of Roberto Clemente.

Major League Baseball named a special award in honor of Clemente, the Roberto Clemente Man of the Year Award given out each year to the baseball player who does the most to help people and his community. It seemed a fitting way to remember one of the greatest men and players to ever play Major League Baseball.

The city of Pittsburgh built a statue of Clemente batting and put it in front of Three Rivers Stadium in 1994. The city also named a bridge after Clemente. The bridge crosses a river leading to the stadium. In addition, schools in Puerto Rico, Pittsburgh, and around the United States have been named after the sports hero.

The Roberto Clemente statue was unveiled outside of Three Rivers Stadium in 1994. Many baseball fans come to honor the memory of "The Great One."

Perhaps the most important way Clemente has been honored is by the opening of his long-dreamed-of sports center. "It is the biggest ambition of my life," Clemente once said of his vision for a huge city of sports. "It will be open to everybody. No matter who they are. . . . I will do this thing because this is what God meant me to do. Baseball is just something that gave me the chance to do this."

Fifteen years after Clemente died, the Roberto Clemente Sports City was inaugurated outside of San Juan, near where Clemente had grown up and first learned to play. The complex has six baseball diamonds, several basketball and tennis courts, and large areas where kids of all ages and abilities can play and learn

A group of Little Leaguers play in Puerto Rico, where baseball remains a large part of everyday life.

from real professional athletes. The site also features places to play soccer and volleyball and to swim.

The death of Clemente helped make the Sports City a reality as governments, people, and corporations felt moved to donate money to honor Clemente. Some of the kids that the Sports City helped, such as Ruben Sierra and Dickie Thon, have even gone on to play Major League Baseball. Both players later wore uniform number 21 in honor of Clemente.

Each year on the anniversary of his death, Clemente's family and friends honor Clemente's memory in their own, private way. They gather on the beach in San Juan to toss flowers into the sea where he disappeared and remember the greatest baseball player to ever come out of Latin America. And more important, they remember the man as much as the player.

In 1971 Major League Baseball created the Commissioner's Award. The following year, after Roberto Clemente's death, the name was changed to the Roberto Clemente Man of the Year Award. The award recognizes the player who, that year, best represents the values Clemente was known for—sportsmanship, community involvement, and being a team player. At the Hall of Fame induction ceremony that year, at which Clemente was inducted, baseball commissioner Bowie Kuhn announced the change.

Each team nominates one player for the award each September. The winner is then selected during the World Series by a panel of distinguished baseball people, including Clemente's widow, Vera, and the commissioner of baseball.

The 2003 winner was pitcher Jamie Moyer of the Seattle Mariners. He and his wife, through their Moyer Foundation established in 2000, have raised almost $3 million to support one hundred different organizations. The foundation helps children and families who are enduring physical, emotional, or financial problems.

Moyer joins some of the greatest players in the history of the game to have been named Man of the Year. In 1999 Tony Gwynn of the San Diego Padres, a future Hall of Famer, won. The year before that, Sammy Sosa of the

MAN OF THE YEAR AWARD

Chicago Cubs was the winner. Other past winners include Cal Ripken Jr. of the Baltimore Orioles, Ozzie Smith of the Saint Louis Cardinals, and Kirby Puckett of the Minnesota Twins. Below is a complete list of winners.

2003 Jamie Moyer

2002 Jim Thome

2001 Curt Schilling

2000 Al Leiter

1999 Tony Gwynn

1998 Sammy Sosa

1997 Eric Davis

1996 Kirby Puckett

1995 Ozzie Smith

1994 Dave Winfield

1993 Barry Larkin

1992 Cal Ripken Jr.

1991 Harold Reynolds

1990 Dave Stewart

1989 Gary Carter

1988 Dale Murphy

1987 Rick Sutcliffe

1986 Garry Maddox

1985 Don Baylor

1984 Ron Guidry

1983 Cecil Cooper

1982 Ken Singleton

1981 Steve Garvey

1980 Phil Niekro

1979 Andre Thornton

1978 Greg Luzinski

1977 Rod Carew

1976 Pete Rose

1975 Lou Brock

1974 Willie Stargell

1973 Al Kaline

1972 Brooks Robinson

1971 Willie Mays

CAREER STATISTICS

YEAR	TEAM	LG	G	AB	R	H	2B	3B	HR	RBI	BB	SO	SB	CS	BA
1955	PIT	N	124	474	48	121	23	11	5	47	18	60	2	5	.255
1956	PIT	N	147	543	66	169	30	7	7	60	13	58	6	6	.311
1957	PIT	N	111	451	42	114	17	7	4	30	23	45	0	4	.253
1958	PIT	N	140	519	69	150	24	10	6	50	31	41	8	2	.289
1959	PIT	N	105	432	60	128	17	7	4	50	15	51	2	3	.296
1960	PIT	N	144	570	89	179	22	6	16	94	39	72	4	5	.314
1961	PIT	N	146	572	100	201	30	10	23	89	35	59	4	1	.351
1962	PIT	N	144	538	95	168	28	9	10	74	35	73	6	4	.312
1963	PIT	N	152	600	77	192	23	8	17	76	31	64	12	2	.320
1964	PIT	N	155	622	95	211	40	7	12	87	51	87	5	2	**.339**
1965	PIT	N	152	589	91	194	21	14	10	65	43	78	8	0	**.329**
1966	PIT	N	154	638	105	202	31	11	29	119	46	109	7	5	.317
1967	PIT	N	147	585	103	**209**	26	10	23	110	41	103	9	1	**.357**
1968	PIT	N	132	502	74	146	18	12	18	57	51	77	2	3	.291
1969	PIT	N	138	507	87	175	20	**12**	19	91	56	73	4	1	.345
1970	PIT	N	108	412	65	145	22	10	14	60	38	66	3	0	.352
1971	PIT	N	132	522	82	178	29	8	13	86	26	65	1	2	.341
1972	PIT	N	102	378	68	118	19	7	10	60	29	49	0	0	.312

Career Totals:

	G	AB	R	H	2B	3B	HR	RBI	BB	SO	SB	CS	BA
18 Seasons	2433	9454	1416	3000	440	166	240	1305	621	1230	83	46	**.317**

Bold stats indicate he led all Major League baseball players in that category
[Source: ESPN.com]

Awards Won
by Roberto Clemente

1961:   National League Gold Glove at OF

1962:   National League Gold Glove at OF

1963:   National League Gold Glove at OF

1964:   National League Gold Glove at OF

1965:   National League Gold Glove at OF

1966:   National League Gold Glove at OF

1966:   National League Most Valuable Player

1967:   National League Gold Glove at OF

1968:   National League Gold Glove at OF

1969:   National League Gold Glove at OF

1970:   National League Gold Glove at OF

1971:   National League Gold Glove at OF

1971:   World Series Most Valuable Player

1972:   National League Gold Glove at OF

TIMELINE

1934 Roberto Walker Clemente is born on August 18.

1947 The Brooklyn Dodgers sign Jackie Robinson, the first African American to play in the major leagues.

1948 Clemente is discovered by softball team manager Roberto Marin, who signs him to play for his Sello Rojo team.

1950 Clemente signs with the amateur baseball team, Juncos.

1952 Clemente tries out for the Dodgers. That same year, Clemente signs his first professional baseball contract and begins playing right field for the Santurce Crabbers.

1954 Clemente signs with the Dodgers on February 19. That summer he plays for the Dodgers' Triple-A team, the Montreal Royals. That winter Branch Rickey signs Clemente to the Pittsburgh Pirates.

1955 Clemente and the Santurce Crabbers win the winter league Caribbean World Series. On April 17, Clemente starts his first game for the Pirates and gets a hit in his first major-league at bat.

1960 The Pirates, led by Clemente, defeat the New York Yankees in the World Series.

1961 Clemente bats .351 and wins the batting title. He also wins his first of many Gold Glove awards as the best fielder at his position and goes to his first All-Star Game.

1963 Clemente meets Vera Cristina Zabala in Puerto Rico during the baseball off-season.

1964 Clemente marries Vera on November 14.

1964-65 Clemente organizes and hosts several baseball clinics for underprivileged kids in Puerto Rico.

1966 After batting .317, swatting 29 home runs, and driving in 119 runs, Clemente wins the National League Most Valuable Player award.

1970 The Pirates open their new ballpark, Three Rivers Stadium. They also honor Clemente by holding Roberto Clemente Night.

1971 On September 1, the Pirates field the first all-black lineup in Major League Baseball history. That fall the Pirates defeat the Baltimore Orioles in the World Series, the first Series to feature televised night games. Clemente is named Series Most Valuable Player.

1972 Clemente gets the 3,000th hit of his career on September 30, in his last at bat of the last game of the year. On December 23, an earthquake hits Managua, Nicaragua, killing more than two thousand people and injuring twenty thousand more. On December 31, bringing supplies to Nicaraguan earthquake victims, Clemente's plane crashes and he dies.

1973 Clemente is voted into the National Baseball Hall of Fame on March 20. On April 5, the Pirates retire Clemente's number 21. The Commissioner's Award is renamed the Roberto Clemente Man of the Year Award.

Source Notes

18   Bill Littlefield and Bernie Fuchs, *Champions: Stories of Ten Remarkable Athletes* (Boston: Little, Brown & Co., 1993), 118.

31   Ibid., 120.

35   Paul Robert Walker, *The Pride of Puerto Rico: The Life of Roberto Clemente* (San Diego: Harcourt Brace and Co., 1988), 44.

50   Littlefield and Fuchs, 125.

58   Bruce Markusen, *Roberto Clemente: The Great One* (Champagne, IL: Sports Publishing Inc., 1998), 124.

63   Ibid., 157.

66   Walker, 124–125.

92   Ibid., 148.

94–95   Ibid., 151.

100   Ibid., 142.

Selected Bibliography

Dunham, Montrew. *Roberto Clemente: Young Baseball Player.* New York: Aladdin Paperbacks, 1997.

Krull, Kathleen. *Lives of the Athletes.* San Diego: Harcourt Brace & Co., 1997.

Littlefield, Bill, and Bernie Fuchs. *Champions: Stories of Ten Remarkable Athletes.* Boston: Little, Brown & Co., 1993.

Markusen, Bruce. *Roberto Clemente: The Great One.* Champagne, IL: Sports Publishing Inc., 1998.

Walker, Paul Robert. *The Pride of Puerto Rico: The Life of Roberto Clemente.* San Diego: Harcourt Brace and Co., 1988.

FURTHER READING AND WEBSITES

Books

Gilbert, Thomas W. *Roberto Clemente*. New York: Chelsea House Publishers, 1995.

Kingsbury, Robert. *Roberto Clemente*. New York: Rosen Central, 2003.

Spalding, Greg. *Sailing the Three Rivers to the Title: Pittsburgh's 1971 Voyage of the Pirate Ship*. Chapel Hill, NC: Professional Press, 1994.

Tagliaferro, Linda. *Puerto Rico in Pictures*. Minneapolis: Lerner Publications Company, 2004.

Websites

Major League Baseball: The Official Site
http://www.mlb.com
The official site of Major League Baseball provides news, photos, video, and statistics on current teams, players, and games. It also has a special kids section and a history section where visitors can learn more about Roberto Clemente and other stars of the past.

National Baseball Hall of Fame and Museum
http://www.baseballhalloffame.org
This website has exhibits and artifacts from baseball's storied history as well as information about all of the Hall of Famers.

The Official Roberto Clemente Website
http://www.robertoclemente21.com
This website provides stories, highlights, and photos from the career and life of the Great One. Visitors can also get more information about the City of Sports, the Roberto Clemente Award, and more.

INDEX